Everybody
Got a
Gift

New and Selected Poems

Everybody Got a Gift

New and Selected Poems

GRACE NICHOLS

A & C Black • London

First published 2005 by
A & C Black Publishers Ltd
37 Soho Square, London, W1D 3QZ

www.acblack.com

ISBN 0 7136 7375 3

A CIP catalogue for this book is available from
the British Library.

Printed and bound in Great Britain by
The Cromwell Press, Trowbridge, Wiltshire

Contents

MOON STRUCK

BETWEEN WEATHERS

THE WORLD OUT THERE

Everybody
Got a
Gift

Everybody Got a Gift

Everybody got a gift
which they bring to the world.
Everybody got a gift,
both boy and girl.

Some have a gift for singing,
let them take their path,
even if the only hit they make
is singing in the bath.

Some have a gift for laughter,
they can crack you up –
make you laugh and laugh
till you think you're gonna pop.

This one brings style,
a cool trend-setter.
Comes on a bad hair day
to help you look better.

Another's good at cooking,
an Ace in the kitchen,
whatever the dish –
just tastes fingerlicking.

That one's got green fingers.
Let green fingers be,
potting and planting.
Look, a little Bonsai Tree.

Everybody got a gift
which they bring to the world.
Everybody got a gift,
start spreading the word.

Little Dancer

Now you must put
your sinewy toes
to their hardest test.

Take a deep breath,
little dancer;
take a deep breath.

Before you burst
into butterfly
from the tight

Cocoon of your dress.

Inspired by the sculpture *Little Dancer Aged Fourteen*
by Edgar Degas, Tate Britain

Waiting For Halley's Comet

Hungry for heavenly bodies, we bundled
from sleep to find a bit of a summit
so we could see Halley's Comet.

But no gleam of Excalibur greeted our eyes,
just a sprinkling of small indifferent stars.
Undaunted we watched the misty skies.

Whatever happened to Halley's Comet?
Whatever happened to that old streaking magnet
making its perihelion passage?

Eventually we trundled back to bed
feeling a right bunch of comics
at not seeing Halley's Comet.

O well, just another seventy-five years to wait.

Give Yourself a Hug

Give yourself a hug
when you feel unloved

Give yourself a hug
when people put on airs
to make you feel a bug

Give yourself a hug
when everyone seems to give you
a cold-shoulder shrug

Give yourself a hug –
a big big hug

And keep on singing,
'Only one in a million like me
Only one in a million-billion-thrillion-zillion
like me.'

Teenage Earthbirds

Flying by
on the winged-wheels
of their heels

Two teenage earthbirds
skateboarding
down the street

Rising
unfeathered –
in sudden air-leap

Defying law
death and gravity
as they do an ollie

Landing back
in the smooth swoop
of youth

And faces gaping,
gawking, impressed
and unimpressed

Only mother watches – heartbeat in her mouth.

Cat-Rap

Lying on the sofa
all curled and meek
but in my furry-fuzzy head
there's a rapping beat.
Gonna rap while I'm napping
and looking sweet
gonna rap while I'm padding
on the balls of my feet

Gonna rap on my head
gonna rap on my tail
gonna rap on my
you know where.
So wave your paws in the air
like you just don't care
with nine lives to spare
gimme five right here.

Well, they say that we cats
are killed by curiosity,
but does the moggie mind?
No, I've got suavity.
When I get to heaven
gonna rap with Macavity,
gonna find his hidden paw
and clear up that mystery.

Nap it up
scratch it up
the knack is free
fur it up
purr it up
yes that's me.

The meanest cat-rapper you'll ever see.
Number one of the street-sound galaxy.

How's That For a Hat?

Mrs Cooper is a hat-fanatic.
Every hat she sees she has to have it.
Who knows how she got this hat-habit?
The salesgirls aren't impressed by her antics.

High hats, low hats,
fat hats, skinny hats,
springy hats, frilly hats,
cocky hats, floppy hats.
Hats in hat-boxes, hats on hat-racks,
hats for opera, hats for race tracks.

'How's that for a hat?' she'll say to you,
whenever she wears a hat that is new.
If you value the friendship of Mrs Cooper
simply answer, 'It's super-duper.'

When My Friend Anita Runs

When my friend Anita runs
she runs straight into the headalong –
legs flashing over grass, daisies, mounds.

When my friend Anita runs
she sticks out her chest like an Olympic
champion – face all serious concentration.

And you'll never catch her looking around,
until she flies into the invisible tape
that says, she's won.

Then she turns to give me
this big grin and hug

O to be able to run like Anita
run like Anita,
Who runs like a cheetah.
If only, just for once, I could beat her.

Book-Heart

The books I love
are well fingered and thumbed
have tiny butter smudges
may harbour a crumb
the odd cat-whisker
a few dog-ears
a drop of tear
a brownish stain
(that looks suspiciously like tea)

I for one, am glad to say,
do not judge a book
by its cover –
but flit first among its leaves
like a hummingbird
sipping at a flower

The books I love I must admit
do not sit with perfect spines
behind a museum of glass.
No the books I love
get kissed and squeezed
and pressed against my heart.

Not Living Up to My Name

I have a terrible reaction
to decimals and fractions

The hypotenuse
leaves me even more obtuse

The isosceles
brings on my allergies

The quadratic equation
gives me a quaking sensation

I worry a great deal
about my brain cells

So any questions about Maths
I'd rather pass

Why on earth did my parents
name me Pythagoras?

The Albatross and the Cat

While the cat just sleeps
in a huddly hold

The albatross sweeps
down an abyss of rock and foam

While the cat just dreams
in a cushiony world

The albatross weeps
for those whose stories are untold

It has seen mushroom clouds
It has heard echoes of human howls

And the cat sleeps on in a cuddly lap.
Dreaming of world peace? Perhaps?

For Forest

Forest could keep secrets
Forest could keep secrets

Forest tune in every day
to watersound and birdsound
Forest letting her hair down
to the teeming creeping of her forest-ground

But Forest don't broadcast her business
no Forest cover her business down
from sky and fast-eye sun
and when night come
and darkness wrap her like a gown
Forest is a bad-dream woman

Forest dreaming about mountain
and when earth was young
Forest dreaming of the caress of gold
Forest rootsing with mysterious Eldorado

and when howler monkey
wake her up with howl
Forest just stretch and stir
to a new day of sound

but coming back to secrets
Forest could keep secrets
Forest could keep secrets

And we must keep Forest.

Cuckoo to You

Haven't you heard
O haven't you heard?
The Cuckoo lays her eggs
in the nests of other birds!
Sounds absurd?

Some people think this bird
is a travesty of mother nature.
Doesn't a pig look after her litter?
But I think Cuckoo is rather clever
for she gets herself a free babysitter.

The Good Old Days

Granny Granny
Please Comb My Hair

Granny Granny please comb my hair
you always take your time
you always take such care

You put me on a cushion between your knees
you rub a little coconut oil
parting gentle as a breeze

Mummy Mummy
she's always in a hurry-hurry
rush
she pulls my hair
sometimes she tugs

But Granny
you have all the time
in the world
and when you're finished
you always turn my head and say,
'Now who's a nice girl?'

The Good Old Days

Grandma is always going on
about the good old days:

Folk were friendlier
Cows were healthier
Stars were brighter
Sun was kinder
Grass was greener
Sugar was sweeter
Sleep was deeper
Food was cheaper
Roses were redder
Children were better

OK, Grandma, but remember while you rave
about the good old days

Your dinner's ready in the microwave.

Cat-Happy

Full of your own content
you leap into my lap
wanting to be stroked and tickled
and sneak a cat-happy nap

O but you're so many things, my cat –
a teacher, a thinker,
a starer, a blinker,
the finest of yoga instructors.
A prowler, a growler, a presiding power,
a staunch and true little sympathiser.
A schemer, a healer, a nine-lives dreamer,
a nifty claw-keen embroiderer
(though I'd prefer if this skill wasn't used on my
sofa)
I could go on –

But right now you're just a baby in fur –
all appreciative purrs
for the gift of a good lunch
and that bright ball of wool we call the sun.

Listening to My Big Sister's Denim Rave

Hey, what's this
at the bottom
of the clothes-pile?

My old shelter-in-a-storm,
my torn fashion-saviour
the number-one style
in which I can't go wrong.

No matter the fray
No matter the rip
No matter the stain
No matter the split
with a bit of lipstick
could even look chic.

Well, watch me
slip/zip/trip
in my old denims
watch me
slide/stride/glide
in my old denims
watch me
dance/prance/advance

Who can stop me when
I take my street-cred stance?

Wha Me Mudder Do

Mek me tell you wha me mudder do
wha me mudder do
wha me mudder do

Me mudder pound plaintain mek fufu
Me mudder catch crab mek calaloo stew

Mek me tell you wha me mudder do
wha me mudder do
wha me mudder do

Me mudder beat hammer
Me mudder turn screw
she paint chair red
then she paint it blue

Mek me tell you wha me mudder do
wha me mudder do
wha me mudder do

Me mudder chase bad-cow
with one 'shoo'
she paddle down river
in she own canoe
Ain't have nothing
dat me mudder can't do
Ain't have nothing
dat me mudder can't do

Mek me tell you.

Moody Mister Sometimish

Sometimish Mister Sometimish
you too sometimish

Sometimish you tipping you cap
with a smile

Sometimish you making you face
sour like lime

Sometimish you stopping for a chat
Sometimish you passing just like that

Sometimish you walking head-in-air
But Mister Sometimish you think I care?

Playing you ain't hearing my howdydo
Mister Sometimish I can be sometimish too

Because you too sometimish Mister Sometimish
Man, you too sometimish.

Humpty

Humpty Dumpty did sit on a wall
Humpty Dumpty did have a great fall
All the King's horses and all the King's men
Did try to put him together again.

But after they left
And poor Humpty had wept
Along came little Hugh
Who knew of super-glue

It took him a while
But Humpty Dumpty was back in style
(Now, Humpty's planning to run 'The Mile').
All because of little Hugh
Who fixed him up with super-glue.

Iguana Memory

Saw an iguana once
when I was very small
in our backdam backyard
came rustling across my path

green like moving newleaf sunlight

big like big big lizard
with more legs than centipede
so it seemed to me
and it must have stopped a while
eyes meeting mine
iguana and child locked in a brief
split moment happening
before it went hurrying

for the green of its life.

Be a Butterfly

Don't be a kyatta-pilla
Be a butterfly
old preacher screamed
to illustrate his sermon
of Jesus and the higher life

rivulets of well-earned
sweat sliding down
his muscly mahogany face
in the half-empty school church
we sat shaking with muffling
laughter
watching our mother trying to save
herself from joining the wave

only our father remaining poker face
and afterwards we always went home to
split peas Sunday soup
with dumplings, fufu and pigtail

Don't be a kyatta-pilla
Be a butterfly
Be a butterfly

That was de life preacher
and you was right.

Chocolate Advice

They told me too many chocolates would make
  my teeth rot.
They told me too many chocolates would give me
  spots.
But when I went back to sneak one from the box
You know those grown-ups, believe it or not,
                    had scoffed the lot.

Moon
Struck

Headmistress Moon

I'm headmistress
of this school they call the night.
I float among my star-pupils
who are all very bright.
When I ring my moon-bell,
everyone pays attention,
the lesson begins with a silent spell,
and then a sparkling concentration.

But sometimes I seriously think
of giving up the headship –
retiring to a cosmic retreat
and putting up my blooming feet.

Me and Moon

This is the story of me and moon
going home one dark afternoon –
there it was floating above the trees
a big blimp of an orange balloon.

Moon-struck, I gazed up.
Was it the moon or was it the sun?
A sunset-sun, some great big hand
had tossed back up again?

Heart jumping against my chest
I began to run
angels at my feet
resurrection trumpets

Back home I stared up through the window,
my clammy seven-year-old hands clasped
as I prayed quietly to myself,
'Please God, don't let the world end, not yet.'

Then I heard my mother's voice behind me,
catching me in its net of safety,
bouncing me right back to right,
'What a beautiful big full moon tonight!'

Moon-Gazer

On a moonlight night
when moon is bright
Beware, Beware –

Moon-Gazer man
with his throw-back head
and his open legs
gazing, gazing
up at the moon

Moon-Gazer man
with his seal-skin hair
and his round-eye stare
staring, staring
up at the moon

Moon-Gazer man
standing tall,
lamp-post tall,
just gazing up
at moon eye-ball

But never try to pass
between those open legs
cause Moon-Gazer man
will close them with a snap –
you'll be trapped

Moon-Gazer man
will crush you flat.
Yes, with just one shake
suddenly you'll be –
a human pancake

On a moonlight night
when moon is bright
for goodness' sake
stay home –
and pull your window-curtain tight.

'Moon-Gazer' is a supernatural folk-figure,
extremely tall, who could be seen mostly straddling
roadways on moonlit nights, gazing up at the moon.
It is best to avoid passing between his legs

I Like to Stay Up

I like to stay up
and listen
when big people talking
jumbie stories

I does feel
so tingly and excited
inside me

But when my mother say,
'Girl, time for bed'

Then is when
I does feel a dread

Then is when
I does jump into me bed

Then is when
I does cover up
from me feet to me head

Then is when
I does wish I didn't listen
to no stupid jumbie story

Then is when I does wish I did read
me book instead.

'Jumbie' is a Guyanese word for ghost

Sleeping Out

What it is we cats get up to
when we don't come home?

What do we do? Where do we go?
Bet you humans would like to know.

Do we make a magic circle
recite poetry, dance and chortle?

Do we form an ancient pack
and prey along the railway track?

Do we set the night on fire
eyes emerald, sapphire?

Do we have a brawling, fur-flying,
caterwauling old knees-up?

Do we find a partner
and have a lovey-dovey smooch-up?

Or do I, bit-of-a-loner,
slink off under the warmth
of a parked car for shelter?

That's for me to know and you to wonder.

The Fairmaid and the Girl Who Wanted More *(for Charles Causley)*

'Fairmaid Fairmaid,
standing on your fishtail
just below my window,
hair in a moonglow.

What will you give me
if I return your fairmaid comb,
the golden one I found
beside the ocean's foam?'

'A box of twelve oysters,
each one with a pearl,
a necklace of coral,
this will be yours.'

Still that girl wanted more –
a chest of gold,
a galleon of silver,
all the sea's fine treasure.

So to her ocean-home
a sad fairmaid returned.
But still she yearned for
her precious comb.

As for that girl who wanted more,
she tosses to this day in her sleep
like a frigate in the stormy deep,
like a sea without a shore.

In the Great Womb-Moon

In the great womb-moon
I once did swoon

Time was a millennium
In my mother's belly

There was water
There was tree
There was land
There was me

There was planet
There was star
There was light
There was dark

How I frog-kicked
And I frolicked
Like a cosmic
Little comic...

Then the water subsided,
I was forced out like a morning-star
Into the borders of another world.
I'm not unhappy, but sometimes,
There's a wee mourn in me for the time when –

Time was a millennium
In my mother's belly.

Counting Sleep

I've tried counting sheep
even goats that bleat and frogs that leap
I've tried falling slow-motion into the ocean
and counting the fish in the deep

But I can't seem to slip into sleep
I've tried both the heavenly and earthly approach
cloud-counting star-counting grass-counting
pebble-counting
I've even tried counting with humming:
    'Ten green bottles standing on the wall
    Ten green bottles...'
But no, I don't accidentally fall
with the green ones in a heap

At last – I give up in defeat
I just know I'll never slip into s
              s
                s
                  s
                   z
                   z
                   z
                    l
                     l
                      l
                       e
                        e
                         e
                          e
                           p

Sekhmet

Only the eyes of the cat
can outstare the serpent
Only the eyes of the cat
can outstare the serpent

Ask Great Cat-Goddess Sekhmet,
headpiece, resplendent helmet,
as she guides the sun-barge each night
on its journey through the underworld.

Here, they must get past Great-Serpent,
the one they call, Fearsome Apep,
waiting in the cave of shadows
with his nightly threats of death.

But by the power of her cat's-eyes
she chills him through like malachite,
steering past his fixed fangs
of stalagmites and stalactites.

And once again Great Sekhmet hears
earth-people singing their hymns of praise
as they watch the sun-barge rising
with its golden promise of grain.

Only the eyes of the cat
can outstare the serpent
Only the eyes of the cat
can outstare the serpent.

Goodbye Shalott

I will not miss you island-tower
I will not miss you days,
seen only through a magic mirror.
My feet have longed to touch
again the grass in summer

Goodbye Shalott
Goodbye Shalott

When the mirror showed me sweet Lancelot,
my gaze did turn direct upon his features,
for the boldness of this look,
for the bareness of this pleasure,
I am to become Death's Bride – a cold treasure

Goodbye Shalott
Goodbye Shalott

Down stream I come to meet my lot,
Far away from that
binding mirror.
My heart has always longed
to be as a flowing river.

In a slow boat I come – The Lady of Shalott.
One day I shall break my banks and flood all
Camelot.

Inspired by the painting *The Lady of Shalott* by John William
Waterhouse, Tate Britain, based on the poem by Alfred Tennyson

Mama-Wata

Down by the seaside
when the moon is in bloom
sits Mama-Wata
gazing up at the moon

She sits as she combs
her hair like a loom
she sits as she croons
a sweet kind of tune

But don't go near Mama-Wata
when the moon is in bloom
for sure she will take you
down to your doom.

Gallery-Ghost at the Tate

The Gallery-Ghost is a host with flair,
an art connoisseur who'll show you
which, what and where –
mistress of the art of moving on air.

When she isn't floating
three inches above the gallery floor
to welcome some visitor
through the gallery door

She's gliding down
an Elizabethan corridor
or flitting by Turner
and a reclining Moore.

A friend to all brushstrokes
the Gallery-Ghost
will steer you to what
she wants you to see most.

When you revisit a painting
it's the Gallery-Ghost of course,
gently whisking you back in,
because you've missed something.

The Gallery-Ghost
O the Gallery-Ghost
Her dedication puts others to shame
But whose face is that –
smiling down from an invisible frame?

Between Weathers

Sun Talk

I am the Sun
I'm a distant fire
I'm not for sale
I'm not for hire
I like it when sky is blue
I bring truth to the view

I am the Sun
I'm a distant fire
I don't tell tales
I don't like liars
I wake in the east
I sleep in the west

My friends all say
I'm blindingly honest.

Daffodils

Long-neck ones
Yellow swans
Too soon gone.

Me and Mister Polite

Again and again
we met in the lane.

We met in the sunshine
We met in the rain
We met in the windy
We met in the hail
We met in the misty
And autumn-leaf trail
On harsh days and dark days
On days mild and clear

And if it was raining
He'd say, 'Nice weather for ducks'
And if it was sunny
He'd say, 'Good enough for beach-wear'
And if it was windy
He'd say, 'We could do without that wind'
And if it was nippy
He'd say, 'Nippy today'
And if it was cold-windy-rainy-grey
(which it nearly always was)
He'd say, 'Horrible day'
Or 'Not as good as it was yesterday'

And he'd hurry away with a brief tip of his hat
His rude dog pulling him this way and that.

Stormman

He snatches up
all the little winds
growing big
under the hood of his skin.

He bays at the skies
bringing down thunder
and lightning
on his side.

He works himself up
into a hunger-sucking rage.
With his whirring-eye
and his hurricane-style

With his flapping-fling
and that singeing-sting,
who can stop him
as he comes howling in?

A werewolf of a man,
size like King Kong
so Stormman comes
whittling down.

Picking up the waves he's raised
he bashes the sea-front,
throwing himself about further inland;
battering windows and doors;

Clawing up rooftiles;
and heaven help anything not secure
like dustbin covers!
Stormman just sends them flying like frisbees.

Getting up
in the middle of the night,
I reach to put on the light.
Suddenly –

Stormman knocks out Electricity,
sending me stumbling
back to bed
as if from a Bogey

By morning
all worn-out
a limp thing –
he crawls out back to sea.

But look at the debris.
Look at the countless fallen trees.
The harvest of shambles,
Signing his name everywhere –

Stormman Woz Ere

At the Bottom of the Garden

No, it isn't an old football
grown all shrunken and prickly
because it was left out so long
at the bottom of the garden.

It's only Hedgehog, who,
when she thinks I'm not looking,
unballs herself to move –
like bristling black lightning.

Making My First Snowman In My Mother's Pink Rubber Gloves

I scooped and shaped him lovingly,
I piled and patted best as could be,
though my pink hands were burning me,
I kept on building my first snowman.

I shaped his shoulders and fixed his neck,
I smoothed his face and rounded his head,
though my pink hands were freezing me,
I kept on building my first snowman.

I put the usual carrot in, for the nose,
a banana for a mouth, my two best conkers for
   his eyes,
though my pink hands were killing me,
I kept on building my first snowman.

I threw my Dad's black jacket
to keep the cold from his back,
I stuck on his head the old felt hat,
then I stepped back.

Why was he staring at me with those big eyes?
Why was he so freezingly alive?
Man, why was he looking at me so?
Oh, no,

He wasn't a snowman.
HE WAS A SNOWCROW!

The Girl With Spring In Her Tongue

She spoke in Spring
She spoke in Summer
She spoke in Autumn
But in Winter
It was another matter altogether

As the days got shorter and colder
And the nights longer and older –
like her pet-turtle and hedgehog friends,
her tongue, which had a mind of its own,
also bedded down in hibernation.

But she went about life as normal.
Her friends played with her as usual.
If her teacher asked a question
she would shake her head but keep schtum
and only nodded to her Dad or Mum

Yes, everyone knew the situation
of the girl who would not speak in Winter.
But with the coming of the sun
a flock of words would burst
from the soft nest of her tongue

No one could stop her talking then. No one.

Inspired by a tale from the Native American tradition –
Swampy Cree Indians

Come On Into My Tropical Garden

Come on into my tropical garden
Come on in and have a laugh in
Taste my sugar cake and my pine drink
Come on in please come on in

And yes you can stand up in my hammock,
and breeze out in my trees
you can pick my hibiscus
and kiss my chimpanzees

O you can roll up in the grass
and if you pick up a flea
I'll take you down for a quick dip-wash
in the sea
believe me there's nothing better
for getting rid of a flea
than having a quick dip-wash in the sea

Come on into my tropical garden
Come on in please come on in.

Sea Timeless Song

Hurricane come
and hurricane go
but sea ... sea timeless
sea timeless
sea timeless
sea timeless
sea timeless

Hibiscus bloom
then dry-wither so
but sea ... sea timeless
sea timeless
sea timeless
sea timeless
sea timeless

Tourist come
and tourist go
but sea ... sea timeless
sea timeless
sea timeless
sea timeless
sea timeless.

Parakeets

Parakeets wheel
        screech
            scream
in a flash of green
among the forest trees
sunlight smooth their feathers
cool leaves soothe their foreheads
creeks are there for beaks
lucky little parakeets.

Star Apple

Deepest purple
or pale green white
the star apple is a sweet fruit
with a sweet star-brimming centre
and a turn-back skin
that always left me sweetly
sticky mouth.

Mango

Have a mango
sweet rainwashed
sunripe mango
that the birds themselves
woulda pick
if only they had seen it
a rosy miracle
Here
take it from mih hand.

Crab Dance

Play moonlight
and the red crabs dance
their scuttle-foot dance
on the mud-packed beach

Play moonlight
and the red crabs dance
their side-ways dance
to the soft-sea beat

Play moonlight
and the red crabs dance
their bulb-eye dance
their last crab dance.

Raspberry

It's the rasp
in your berry
that makes us tick.

It's the tang
in the flavour
that gives us a kick.

But raspberry
why does one of
your tiny pulps – all aglow

Remind me so
of a full-blooded
mosquito?

Autumn Song

Rusty-red, yellow,
Brown
Summer's gone,
Winter to come

By the windfall of apples
And the stripping of trees
By the pick-up of conkers
And the carpet of leaves

By the tired-face flowers
And the mould on the mound
By the soles crunching berries
And the bees' farewell-hum

Rusty-red, yellow,
Brown
Summer's gone,
Winter to come.

Mister Goodacre's Garden

The neighbours say he's weird and wicked
Just cause Mister Goodacre won't mow down
His high grass or thicket,
(Their own lawns look ready
for billiards or cricket)

I guess he just loves tall grass waving
I think the length of his dandelions amazing,
But the neighbours keep throwing him these
spearing-looks,
Which seem to say, 'You're lowering the tenor
Of the neighbourhood.'

Mister Goodacre just stands there
Whistling carefree,
Waving a water-gun for all to see;
'Think me lazy,' he says, 'think me crazy,
but I will defend my dandelions and daisies'.

More power to your wild flowers, Mister Goodacre,
But while you're basking...
I'm afraid the neighbours
Are planning a grass-murder
With their lawn-mowers.

Airy Fairy

She was fat
She was airy
A special billowing
kind of fairy
brushing each flower
not with a wand
but with the flowing
plumpness of her hand.

On a morning of spring
I heard her sigh
I heard her sing

O isn't it cheery
to be an airy fairy
frisking from rose to rose
on my fat tippy toes.

Sun Is Laughing

This morning she got up
on the happy side of bed,
pulled back the grey sky-curtains
and poked her head
through the blue window
of heaven,
her yellow laughter
spilling over,
falling broad across the grass,
brightening the washing on the line,
giving more shine
to the back of a ladybug
and buttering up all the world.

Then, without any warning,
as if she was suddenly bored,
or just got sulky
because she could hear no one
giving praise
to her shining ways,
Sun slammed the sky-window close
plunging the whole world
into greyness once more.

O Sun, moody one,
how can we live
without the holiday of your face?

The World
Out
There

Don't Cry, Caterpillar

Don't cry, Caterpillar
Caterpillar, don't cry
You'll be a butterfly – by and by.

Caterpillar, please
Don't worry 'bout a thing

'But,' said Caterpillar,
'will I still know myself – in wings?'

My Gran Visits England

My Gran was a Caribbean lady
As Caribbean as could be
She came across to visit us
In Shoreham by the sea.

She'd hardly put her suitcase down
when she began a digging spree
Out in the back garden
To see what she could see

And she found:
That the ground was as groundy
That the frogs were as froggy
That the earthworms were as worthy

That the weeds were as weedy
That the seeds were as seedy
That the bees were as busy
as those back home

And she paused from her digging
And she wondered
And she looked at her spade
And she pondered.

Then she stood by a rose
As a slug passed by her toes
And she called to my Dad
as she struck pose after pose,

'Boy, come and take my photo – the place cold,
But wherever there's God's earth, I'm at home.'

Morning

Morning comes
  with a milk-float jiggling

Morning comes
  with a milkman whistling

Morning comes
  with empties clinking

Morning comes
  with alarm clock ringing

Morning comes
  with toaster popping

Morning comes
  with letters dropping

Morning comes
  with kettle singing

Morning comes
  with me just listening.

Morning comes to drag me out of bed
  – Boss-Woman Morning.

Chock-a-block

It was chock-a-block.
We were truly stuck
Cars, lorries, buses, trucks,
caught up in a jam called Traffic.
Terrific.

Nothing to do but sit and wait
nothing to do but think I'm late.
'Sorry, mate,' the taxi driver says,
'Vauxhall Bridge is chockers,
absolutely chockers.'

Suddenly I remembered,
what a piece of luck!
Lying in my bag –
a divine milk choc.
And believe it or not

As that choc
melted in my mouth
so did the jam called Traffic.
Thanks to my bar of choc
we're no longer chock-a-block.

For Dilberta
Biggest of the Elephants at London Zoo

The walking-whale
of the Earth kingdom – Dilberta.

The one whose waist
your arms won't get around – Dilberta

The mammoth one whose weight
you pray, won't knock you to the ground.

The one who displays toes
like archway windows,
bringing the pads of her feet down
like giant paperweights
to keep the earth from shifting about.

Dilberta, rippling as she ambles under
the wrinkled tarpaulin of her skin,
casually throwing the arm of her nose,
saying, 'Go on, have a stroke'.

But sometimes, in her mind's eye,
Dilberta gets this idea - She could be a Moth!
Yes, with the wind stirring behind her ears,
she could really fly.

Rising above the boundaries of the paddock,
Making for the dark light of the forest –

Hearing, O once more, the trumpets roar.

Baby-K Rap Rhyme

My name is Baby-K
An dis is my rhyme
Sit back folks
While I rap my mind;

Ah rocking with my homegirl,
My Mommy
Ah rocking with my homeboy,
My Daddy
My big sister, Les, an
My Granny,
Hey dere people – my posse
I'm the business
The ruler of the nursery

poop po-doop
poop-poop po-doop
poop po-doop
poop-poop po-doop

Well, ah soaking up de rhythm
Ah drinking up my tea
Ah bouncing an ah rocking
On my Mommy knee
So happy man so happy

poop po-doop
poop-poop po-doop
poop po-doop
poop-poop po-doop

Wish my rhyme wasn't hard
Wish my rhyme wasn't rough
But sometimes, people
You got to be tough

Cause dey pumping up de chickens
Dey stumping down de trees
Dey messing up de ozones
Dey messing up de seas
Baby-K say, stop dis –
please, please, please

poop po-doop
poop-poop po-doop
poop po-doop
poop-poop po-doop

Now am splashing in de bath
With my rubber duck
Who don't like dis rhyme
Kiss my baby-foot
Babies everywhere
Join a Babyhood

Cause dey hotting up de globe, man
Dey hitting down de seals
Dey killing off de ellies
For dere ivories

Baby-K say, stop dis –
please, please, please

poop po-doop
poop-poop po-doop
poop po-doop
poop-poop po-doop

Dis is my Baby-K rap
But it's a kinda plea
What kinda world
Dey going to leave fuh me?
What kinda world
Dey going to leave fuh me?

Poop po-doop.

The Dissatisfied Poem

I'm a dissatisfied poem
   I really am
there's so many things
   I don't understand
like why I'm lying
   on this flat white page
when there's so much to do
   in the world out there
But sometimes when I catch a glimpse
   of the world outside
it makes my blood curl
   it makes me want to stay inside
and hide
   please turn me quick
before I cry
   they would hate it if I wet the pages.

On the News

So what's new? asks Death
switching on the box –

The flickering life
of a starving child

A bomber heading
for a distant sky

The empty words
of another white paper

So what's new? asks Death
switching off the box

Such a small screen
holding such a wide hunger.

Tabby

My cat is all concentrated tiger.
I can only imagine the thousands
of millions of years
it must have taken to perfect her.
Growing smaller and smaller
with each evolution.
Growing more and more refined
and even-tempered under her fur.

See how she constantly licks
and grooms herself all over?

A small Queen of Sheba
stamping everywhere her padded
signature – a royal reminder
of the days she was a full-blown tiger.
Older O much older than Egypt.

Now, just look at her –
my grey and black tabby, stepping lightly,
emerging head first from between
the green garden stalks –

Ancient and new as the birth of a star.

Gulf Gull

The oil-stricken gull
has struggled ashore,
and although full-grown,
looks like a bewildered
scraggy fledgling.

Her oil-tarred wings
seem heavy as lead
as she totters slightly,
stiff-legged.

Staring out at us
with an unblinking
atomic,
almost comic surprise.

She hasn't taken any sides
but she's lost her natural home
and more. An unanswerable cry
is stuck in her throat
        Why?

Ar-a-rat

I know a rat on Ararat,
He isn't thin, he isn't fat
Never been chased by any cat
Not that rat on Ararat.
He's sitting high on a mountain breeze,
Never tasted any cheese,
Never chewed up any old hot,
Not that rat on Ararat.
He just sits alone on a mountain breeze,
Wonders why the trees are green,
Ponders why the ground is flat,
O that rat on Ararat.
His eyes like saucers, glow in the dark –
The last to slip from Noah's ark.

If I Had a Giraffe

If I had a giraffe –
I'd climb up a ladder to her with a laugh.
I'd rest my head against her long neck,
and we'd go – riding riding riding.

We'd go anywhere under the sky,
maybe to some faraway blue seaside,
just to see flying fish flashing by,
and we'd go – riding riding riding.

We'd go to the land
where all fruit trees grow,
and my giraffe would stretch her neck
to get me to the highest, rosiest mango,
and we'd go – riding riding riding.

Even to the desert where the hot sands glow,
we'd go – riding riding riding.
Me and my beautiful giraffe-friend,
whose face reminds me of a camel.

Learning to Swim *(for Kalera)*

Learning to swim, your girl-walking
land-accustomed body
turns horizontal wriggly

Arms and legs such strange things
like wayward fins
trying to get you from A to B to C

And yes you're learning how to be
a submarine dancer,
a froggie
a floatie
a spirogyra

Kicking through the new
yet familiar element called water.

Colour Reunion

Brother Green, so highly esteemed,
wipes his face in his leafy sleeves.

Sister Yellow, with a burst of laughter,
strokes the canary on her shoulder.

Uncle White stands at the window
remembering his small days in the snow.

Auntie Blue in her satiny cerulean
rolls in like a wave off the Mediterranean

Father Red, a flaming hat on his head,
strolls in looking devilishly dread.

Mother Black with winkling eye
spreads her starry tablecloth from on high

'Grandpa Brown and Grandma Purple
Greatuncle Grey and Greataunt Silver

Not to mention Cousin Mauve and Magenta
They're all coming, yes all coming to dinner.'

Index of Poem Titles

Index of First Lines

Acknowledgements

This collection brings together new poems alongside a
selection from Grace Nichols' previous books, including:
Come On Into My Tropical Garden (A&C Black, 1988);
No Hickory No Dickory No Dock (Viking, 1991);
Give Yourself A Hug (A&C Black, 1994);
Asana And The Animals (Walker Books, 1997);
The Poet Cat (Bloomsbury Children's Books, 2000);
and *Paint Me A Poem* (A&C Black, 2004).